FRINGE

MY LIFE AS A SPIRIT-FILLED CHRISTIAN WITH ASPERGER'S SYNDROME

STEPHANIE MAYBERRY

STEPHANIE A. MAYBERRY

FRINGE
MY LIFE AS A SPIRIT-FILLED CHRISTIAN WITH ASPERGER'S SYNDROME

by

STEPHANIE MAYBERRY

All scriptures used in this text are taken from the New American Standard Bible and the Amplified Bible.

ISBN-13: 978-1466399549

ISBN-10: 1466399546

DEDICATION

Growing up (and even as an adult) I always felt like an alien, an outsider, a misfit. I never felt as if I "fit in" with anyone, not even my family. But when I finally took Jesus' hand, the hand He had been extending to me my whole life, I knew I had found the place where I belonged.

This book is dedicated to those who feel like I did, an alien, an outsider, a misfit. While you may feel as if this world does not have a place for you, you always, always belong in Jesus' family. He accepts you just as you are.

This book is for you.

.

Dear Reader,

If the words in my books speak to you, resonate with you, touch you, please know it isn't really me, it is God speaking to you.

See, I am just a vessel that He uses to convey His message to you, to others. I am no great writer; I am just the obedient hand that holds the pen for the greatest author of all – my God.

He alone deserves all of the praise, all the glory.

Thank you so much for your support and encouragement. Each and every email, every word, every letter is such a treasure to me! I pray for your continued growth in your relationship with God. Forever walk in His Word and you will know blessings beyond your imagination.

God is so good, isn't He?

Stephanie Mayberry

STEPHANIE A. MAYBERRY

CONTENTS

STEPHANIE A. MAYBERRY

ACKNOWLEDGMENTS

I want to especially thank my best friend who also happens to be my husband. CW, you are most definitely one of the most beautiful, special, wonderful gifts God has ever given me. I am so very blessed to have you in my life. You have changed my life in so many ways. You give me a safe place to hide when the world is just too much, you listen, even when I go on and on, you appreciate my honesty and give me the honesty that I so desperately need.

You are my guide, my leader, my friend, my partner, my prayer partner, my protector and my love. Without you, I doubt I would have had the courage to put this on paper. Without you, I would not be in our wonderful church. Without you, I would have never realized the glorious blessing that God bestowed upon me when He brought you into my life. I thank Him every day for bringing you to me.

I love you.

Stephanie Mayberry

STEPHANIE A. MAYBERRY

1

BEFORE WE GET STARTED

It is not an accident that you are reading this. It was not a fluke that led you to pick up this book and begin reading these words. No, God has something to say to YOU and He led you here. It doesn't matter if you believe or not, God still works in your life. Even if you don't believe in His almighty power, He will still speak to you in whatever way you understand. All you have to do is listen.

Maybe today you didn't realize that you were listening, but here you are! And God has given me a message, a message just for you. Now you may be thinking, "She's crazy! Many people will read this book. How can the message be just for me?" or you may think that because I have Asperger's that I can't possibly understand or communicate the message that God has given me. But all that doesn't matter.

It is simple, really. When God speaks, even to many, even to people who have challenges like mine, whose brain is different, each person hears the individual message – exactly what God wants each individual, special person to hear.

This is the TRUTH. You can't change the truth or manipulate it to fit what you want to believe or what you want it to be. The truth is the truth and that is all there is to it. Please remember that as you read this.

My husband said that when he read this, he laughed out loud in some places. I want you to know that that is OK. People often think I am amusing, even when I don't mean to be (especially then) so I just smile or laugh with them (even though I have no idea why I am laughing – my husband usually explains later). Laughter is good. It creates a good attitude which can bring about acceptance of our differences So if something is funny, laugh.

So people say I should tell you about myself before we really begin. That is hard. I don't know where to start – or where to stop.

2

INTRODUCTION

"Let your light so shine before men, that they may see your good works, and glorify your Father which is in heaven." Matthew 5:16

Most books that I have read that are nonfiction have an introduction. The people who have helped me learn how to be more adept at social interactions told me that I should introduce myself before I talk to people. They say I should let them know a little about me before I really talk to them because it helps them understand me and believe in me.

Anyway, this is my introduction. My name is Stephanie Mayberry. I grew up in Baton Rouge, Louisiana but now I live in Northern Virginia, just outside of Washington, D.C. There has been a lot that has happened in my life, but they also said I don't have to tell everything, just the parts that are relevant to what I am writing here.

So, I think the two most important things you need to know about me (maybe the only things you need to know for this book) are 1) I am a spirit-filled (Apostolic or Pentecostal to be exact) Christian and I love Jesus with my whole heart, and 2) I have Asperger's Syndrome. Asperger's (AS) is a form of autism. Some doctors call it an "invisible disability" because I don't limp and I am not disfigured, but I have some difficult challenges just the same.

To look at me, you wouldn't think anything was different about me probably. I look like everyone else. When I talk to people, I can usually do a pretty good job of seeming normal because I took a lot of courses in high school and college that taught me the technical aspects of communication (even though back then I did not know that my difficulty was because I have Asperger's). I have studied sociology and psychology as well. I just want to fit in – but I never have. See, most people with Asperger's have limited social functioning. I don't have the emotional element that most people have, especially when I am talking to someone. I don't get hints, don't understand what they call "social nuances" (I say the term, but even still do not know what it is). I don't understand people and social encounters are very difficult and stressful for me.

I will explain more about how AS affects me (it affects different people in different ways) in a later chapter. Now I think I need to explain to you how this book came to be.

See, God had placed this book on my heart. He wanted me to write it, but He was only giving me bits and pieces of the whole picture (probably because I see best when I can see just the individual pieces of something – the "big picture" as they call it is hard for me to see). I prayed about it, I ignored it a lot. I started portions but did it my way and not the way that God was guiding me. The more pieces that I saw, the scarier it was to me. It just looked too big, too important and I didn't think I was qualified.

Yet, everywhere I went, people were pointing out to me things like how I could write well, how I could help other people who also have Asperger's and how I could reach out and help people who had a friend or family member with Asperger's – how I could help other people know Jesus better. It wasn't just the people I knew, random people, people I met on the subway or on the bus, were also telling me these things.

Now, understand, I am not a social person, but I was taught that you should be friendly. I know the technical part of being friendly, smile, greet the person, say something nice. I have hundreds of scripts in my head that help me with these impromptu encounters. I listen to what the person says and usually I have a script in my head that goes with what they are saying. I recite it and the encounter is usually over before the script runs out. Not always, but usually.

I don't go out seeking random strangers to talk to, people make me nervous. But people certainly come looking for me! They are really nice most of the time. We talk and usually I just let them tell me about themselves and they like that. I like it too because I can learn more about them and about people. I have met some of the most extraordinary everyday people!

But now I want to tell you about how I started writing this book and why it is this book.

There is someone in my life, someone close to me, who has hurt me repeatedly. I have tried to make peace with them. I have talked about it with them and with other people, prayed about it and tried really hard to forgive this person and make peace between us. Still, I feel the pain, the distrust, the sadness and grief that all come from the wrongs that I feel this person has done to me.

It seems that just as we do come to some sort of peace, when I begin to relax, they do something cruel and hurtful again. I don't understand it. But, like I said, I don't understand people.

So, one sweltering Sunday afternoon in July (Don't ever let anyone tell you that "way up in Virginia" does not get H-O-T. It does!) I sat thinking about the sermon our pastor preached that morning. It was about how the devil heats things up, tries to trip us up in an effort to prevent us from accomplishing the missions that God lays on our hearts. For several years, God had been working on me, prodding me to use the gifts that he gave me to help others. I felt him pressing me to write. There were several areas, he even provided me with the relevant scripture! All he wanted me to do was sit down and write the words that he was placing on my heart.

But I had a million and one excuses. I was tired, working too hard, too busy with the kids, distracted by household duties, stressed out, there was no end to the reasons I could come up with to not do what God wanted me to do. But He kept on.

And one by one, the things I claimed were keeping me from doing what He wanted began to disappear. I was sleeping very well and waking feeling refreshed and, well, pretty fantastic. Several people in my office who were stressing me out got new jobs. My workload decreased and I got home much less tired. As my list got shorter and shorter, I began to feel the heat.

But I still had the kids. Now, granted, they were teenagers and pretty self sufficient, but they still needed their mom. Then, lo and behold, I had room in the budget to send them to visit their family, lots of family, for two months. So off they went and there I sat.

I was all out of excuses.

"God wants me to write." I told my husband one morning as we sat drinking our coffee. We are early birds, up by 4 AM on weekdays and rarely sleeping past 6 AM on the weekends. My husband is my best friend, a wonderful, Godly man and has wisdom that astounds me.

"Hmm." He responded, looking out into the predawn darkness, "When are you going to start?" It never was a question of whether I would do it or not, just when was I going to start. So, I started thinking about it. I didn't really sit down and actually write anything for a while. But I was closer than I had ever been. I began praying about it and God began working in me.

That's about the time that the devil got involved. I suppose he saw me getting pretty close to doing what God was asking of me. I was also getting more spiritual, closer to God and I guess that just didn't sit right with him because that is when my world seemed to blow completely apart. No sense in rehashing it all here, just suffice it to say that people I trusted, believed in, let me down. They deceived me and hurt me.

Funny, things seemed to settle, but the very day the whole picture of this project God wanted me to do came into focus, this situation with these people spun out of control. I had finally put all the pieces together, formatted this manuscript and had begun writing. I had even realized why the word "Fringe" kept rolling around in my head as the title. The events that unfolded coincided almost perfectly with my actions of developing this manuscript and I can only describe them as demonic driven. It was obvious something was trying to stop me.

And, I am sorry to say, it did stop me. For three days I was emotionally paralyzed, unable to focus, crying, wishing I could die and leave it all behind. Then that Thursday morning I woke feeling physically terrible. I had a headache I could not relieve; my stomach was upset, I was dizzy and felt lousy. I saw my husband off to work, called in to my own work to let them know I would not be in, then went and lay back down. But I could not rest.

I kept thinking of the situation that had escalated so much in the previous days. Then somewhere through the pain and heartache that was debilitating me, I felt a stirring. I had to write. This was not a desire to write, or even a need, but a strong, definite command to write. I had no choice. So I got out of bed, opened my laptop and obeyed.

I thank God again and again for bringing my husband into my life. His support was and is invaluable. He was so loving, so supportive. Had I been forced to go through it all alone, I am not sure I would have fared as well.

3

WHY FRINGE?

"You are the light of the world…" Matthew 5:14

As God was pressing on me to write this, as it began to take shape, a single word kept repeating over and over in my head. Fringe. But the only pictures I saw were bright light. I was confused. I only know of fringe as the strings that hang off of the edge of fabric. I also have heard people use the word to describe people who did not do things "normal" or they did radical things their own way. But I could not make the connection between the pictures of light I was seeing and the word I kept hearing. It made no sense.

Before we go further, I should explain to you that I think in pictures. I don't see words or nothingness when I hear words. I see pictures that illustrate the words. For instance, when someone says something is "over the top" I see someone jumping over a big, red and white tent (what they call a big top in the circus). When someone says a person "bought the farm" I see a farmer in overalls paying a man in a suit for a red barn with pigs and cows.

Can you see how this could get very confusing when trying to communicate with someone?

Anyway, the word and the picture were not making sense together. I could not see the connection. I started to think that maybe I was confused. Maybe I had heard the word somewhere and I just liked the sound of it (I do – it feels good to think but I don't like to say it cause it feels funny when it leaves my mouth). Maybe I was picturing the light because I think of God as light in a dark world. Maybe, as they say, I was getting my signals crossed. Then, on that day I told you about, that day I actually started writing this, that day those people started attacking and hurting me, I looked up fringe in the dictionary.

There were the usual definitions about the outer border of something, decorative border and social groups that hold views that are beyond what is considered normal or socially acceptable. Then, there it was, "one of the light or dark bands produced by the interference and diffraction of light."

I looked up "diffraction of light" and learned that it is a term used to describe the behavior of light when it encounters an obstacle. The wave of light (I enjoy thinking of light as waves, it makes me think of water and that is comforting) comes up against an obstacle, but instead of knocking it over or trying to penetrate it, the light simply bends around it. The light yields to the obstacles and instead of fighting them, encompasses them. When this happens, bands of light are produced and they are called fringe.

I want to be fringe.

I want to bring the light that is Jesus, the Word of God to people. When I encounter someone who is resistant, an obstacle to the light, I want to be able to bend around that obstacle, that person, encompassing them in Jesus' light and love. I don't want to fight them or try to force my way in, just wrap the light around them.

Different obstacles react in different ways to different types of light. Some things melt, others turn to vapor, some get harder and some don't change at all. People are like that too. Some will begin to melt (well not really, but they will be more pliable and the Word can get in easier), others will turn to vapor and become the light. And, yes, some will get harder or not change at all, but that is a chance I have to take.

Another thing I found interesting in my research is that refraction of light (the other part of what fringe is) is how our eyes see images. So, not only can we be part of the light that is encompassing obstacles, we are also helping to form and shape the image of God for others to see.

Maybe this seems simplistic, but I don't think that God would make things too terribly complicated for us to understand. He talks to each of us in the way that we best understand. I know this. He talks to me with pictures and a certain type of feeling but I know that He talks to my husband in a completely different way. However, He gives us all the same basic message: Lead others to Him; show them the light and the truth.

We are to be the salt and light of the world. Boy was problematic for me when I first started thinking about it! I saw salt and I saw light but I didn't see how I could turn into salt or become light. My literal mind could not understand that phrasing. Once again, my husband interpreted it for me and explained it so that I could understand. What it comes down to is that we are supposed to bring hope to people, encourage them and help them find peace by introducing them to God and by helping them foster a growing, close relationship with Him. We are supposed to encompass people with the light and teach them how to get to Heaven.

So, yeah, we are supposed to be the fringe. .

4

ASPERGER'S AND ME

"And God created man in His own image, in the image of God." Genesis 1:27

I guess I should explain more about Asperger's Syndrome and, more importantly, how it affects me. See, there is a saying, "If you have seen one person with Asperger's, you have seen one person with Asperger's." This means that the condition presents itself in many different ways. So, this is Asperger's Syndrome from my perspective. Understand that I can only speak for myself. Someone else with Asperger's may experience it in a completely different way. Also understand that I can only speak about things that I have experienced. If it has not happened to me or I have not encountered it, I cannot talk about it because I don't know how I would react to it.

Asperger's Syndrome is a form of Autism. Granted, it is a high functioning Autism, but it still presents daily challenges to me just the same. It is NOT a mental health issue. Furthermore, it is NOT a psychiatric condition, rather a neurological (brain and nervous system) condition. To put it in elementary terms, my brain is constructed in a way that is vastly different from most people's brains.

You should know that sometimes psychiatric conditions can come from the AS. Anxiety is very common (change upsets some of us, as do social interaction, crowds, and, well, people in general). Some people with AS also get depressed and have some issues with obsessive compulsive disorder. It is hard to say that AS causes these things, but it may be a component because many people with AS do tend to experience these things. Then again many neuro typical (NT) people experience them as well. Who knows?

I don't ask people to treat me differently, but I do ask that they respect my differences as I make numerous accommodations every day to respect the differences that they have from me. For the most part, I tend to just avoid people. I try not to, but sometimes it is just easier. If I am feeling stressed or overwhelmed, people make me more nervous.

It is a common trait among people with Asperger's to be extremely loyal and honest. Those who extend kindness and acceptance (it doesn't even have to be understanding – I don't expect you to understand me any more than I understand you) are often rewarded with fierce loyalty and a hard, dependable worker. I may be rather quiet, shy, even introverted, but if you need me, I will be there for you.

A bad thing, though, is that people with AS have a hard time understanding that not everyone who is nice to them is their friend. They think that if a person is kind to them then that person is their friend. We don't understand relationships, how bonds grow or love develops (I still don't understand all of that even though I am married). If you are kind to me, you are my friend and I will be loyal, honest and a devoted friend to you.

People have hurt me time and again, but then they are nice to me and I believe that they are my friend. I don't understand how or why someone would do something bad to a friend, but that is what happens. I get sad, sometimes I feel scared and I feel very frustrated because I don't understand. There are some people who have stayed by me and not tried to hurt me on purpose. My husband, CW, is one of those people. He is always there for me and is my best friend. My friend, Paige is another. I have known her since we were 3 years old. We have disagreed, but we always come back to being friends and she would not try to harm me. Even people in my family have tried to hurt me or not helped protect me from being hurt. I have learned that some people only care about themselves and will let someone else get hurt if it means that they themselves won't get hurt. I don't think that is a real friend.

When people interrupt me or talk over me when it is my turn to speak it upsets me. This behavior is inappropriate, is ineffective communication and is not conducive to effective conflict resolution. It is very distressing because in a conversation everyone should have a chance to speak without being interrupted.

When someone yells at me, raises their voice to me, launches a verbal assault upon me or attempts to communicate with me in an emotionally charged, agitated manner it is difficult for me to process the words. Actually, I don't really hear them, not in a logical, flowing manner that makes any sense to me. While I may pick up a word here or there, to me, all the yelling and increased inflection in their voice is nothing but gibberish. I don't hear what they are saying and, more importantly, understand what they are attempting to communicate to me. All I hear is a lot of noise.

Little things that will help you understand me (in relation to the Asperger's):

- I am very logical

- I don't understand emotions, not the way that NTs do

- Emotional outbursts make no sense to me, they make a person's face change shape and they sound different. Usually I can't understand their words.

- I don't understand nonverbal communication. While I may note something, a gesture or facial expression, I am usually unable to process it or understand it if I have not had experience with it in the past. You may as well be speaking to me in a foreign language. I understand best when people say what they mean and speak literally.

- I am literal. I say what I mean and mean what I say. I have no underlying motives, no hidden agendas. I do what needs to be done and say what needs to be said. If you want an honest answer, ask me. But first make absolutely certain that you want the truth.

- I may make mistakes but I <u>DO NOT</u> lie! It is highly offensive when I am accused of such. I get very upset if I am lied to, lied about or accused of lying. I will tell the truth, no matter what. If you have a question, just ask me and I will give you an honest, straightforward answer, simple as that.

- I have a strong sense of what is right and just. Fairness is very important; justice is vital.

- I like structure.

- I am fascinated with patterns and numbers. Everything has a pattern if you look close enough.

- I like symmetry. When things are uneven it is upsetting.

- I like things to be the way they are supposed to be.

- Choices are very hard for me. I struggle with making selections off of a menu and grocery shopping is difficult too. I read all of the labels and make deliberate, analytical comparisons between brands, variations of the product, sizes and prices. I want to make the perfect choice. That isn't easy at all.

- I have a hard time understanding or processing voices when there are a lot of other voices or other noises.

- I am not very social and do not understand "small talk" or its purpose. Why ask, "How are you?" if you don't really want to know? When I answer people who ask this and tell the truth (If I am not OK, I can't say that I am, that would be a lie) they usually seem uncomfortable or nervous (It is really hard to tell but I know it is something because they start moving around, shift from one foot to the other and they look all around).

- When I am on a job or project, that task is my first priority. Social functions and frivolous interactions (whether it is going to get coffee with an officemate or attending a party) are secondary priorities.

- I am not good with eye contact. Some people are just hard to look at (this is especially true if they are upset with me or are very emotional), but most of the time, it is just hard to make eye contact. I understand that this is common among people with AS, but knowing that doesn't really help me much because people don't understand. A lot of people think I am not telling the truth or hiding something but I am not, I just can't look someone in the eye for too long. And the trick that the books say about focusing on the person's forehead so that it looks like you are looking them in the eye is silly. I won't do that, it is a lie; it is deceitful and I am not like that.

- I am dumb in some ways (social) and smart in other ways (organizing large amounts of data and finding connections between things that don't seem to be related). But I do know that God made me this way for a reason. So I just do my best. I focus on living for Him and try really hard to be like Jesus. That's really all I can do.

Because verbal communication is so difficult for me to understand sometimes (especially when it is very loud like yelling or very emotional), I prefer written communication. If someone has something important to say to me, it is best to do it in writing. Brief, concise (preferable bulleted) items are best for me. I prefer to stick to the facts and allow logic to prevail with limited emotion (because I don't understand the emotional component and it only serves to cloud my ability to process, further frustrating me and making the problem worse).

Many people with AS are sensory defensive. I am sensory defensive. This means that my brain takes in all sensory input (to which I am sensitive – sound is the worst) and is unable to filter out unimportant messages from the important ones. In short, I hear everything. It is very distracting and stressful because it puts my entire system in a hyper-alert state. It is particularly true when it comes to certain sounds (the vacuum cleaner, noisy food, fans, high pitched or loud voices). It is best to speak to me in a normal or low tone and stay calm.

These things can make church very difficult for me. When there are a lot of sounds and things going on at the same time (several people praying, music, lights low or dim, the projection screen flickering and people singing) it can be overwhelming and very distracting. I feel overwhelmed and sometimes it is even somewhat uncomfortable. When there is too much going on it is very hard to concentrate and sometimes it is even hard to breathe (if it is hot, it is even worse). My mind can't stay focused on one thing and I have a really, really hard time making the connection, especially in prayer. Sometimes I can't do it at all. Most people don't understand that and sometimes I feel like they think bad things about me or they judge me. I think that sometimes people think that because of that or because I am physically uncomfortable raising my arms they think I am not a good or real Christian. That upsets me.

I am different. I can't change that. However, I do feel that God put me here for a reason. He has a purpose for me just as he has a purpose for you. Everything I do, I do for God and everything I am, I am because of God. I may not be able to communicate very well verbally and I may be socially awkward, but that doesn't mean I should be discounted to belittled for my challenges. Most of the time I feel like someone dropped me in the middle of a foreign country and didn't teach me the language or the culture. I am getting by the best that I can. I make blunders and sometimes people think I am strange or I upset them because of things I say or do, but I don't mean to upset anyone. I just want to follow the path that God has for me, do His will and be the person He wants me to be.

God made me so even though I am different from many people, I was still created in His image. The Bible says that. It means that I was created to be like Him, reflect Him, to be spiritually like Him. In that way I am just like everyone else. .

5

PEOPLE

"And you yourself must be an example to them by doing good works of every kind. Let everything you do reflect the integrity and seriousness of your teaching." Titus 2:7

I don't understand people. Some people are nice; some are not nice. Some people pretend to be nice when they are with you, then are not nice and say bad things about you when they aren't with you. People say one thing and mean another. They are emotional and complex and they change a lot. But to me, they are beautiful and fascinating.

I have trouble communicating with people, especially when I talk. I don't understand them because they say things they don't mean, but they also don't understand me because I say what I do mean. They try to relate to me but they use their own neurological functioning as a reference and that doesn't work. My brain works differently from theirs and just as I cannot expect them to approach a situation in the same manner that I would, they cannot expect me to approach a situation the way that they would.

People have trouble understanding me too though. Because I am so socially clumsy (or feel that way), I am very uncomfortable in social situations. Often I avoid them or shrink back out of the limelight. I don't like attention drawn to me (although I don't mind giving my testimony or speaking in front of crowds if I can help or encourage others). People, specifically NTs, often mistake this shyness as aloofness or even snobbishness. They are "put off" by it. They just don't understand me at all. That makes me sad.

If people would just take the time to get to know me, not just superficially, they might find someone they like. People who do know me well do really like me. The trick is, though, getting to really know me. I am shy, awkward and very unsure of myself when it comes to social interactions. Again, these traits make it difficult for me to act in church the way others expect me to or think I should. I have found that many (maybe most) NTs leave very little leeway for me if I am not exactly like them. They expect me to act and think and worship and pray the way that they do and if I don't, they seem to think less of me – or at least think I am less of a Christian.

There are some people who understand or at least accept – a few in my church – but they are few and far between. I have come to realize that finding NTs who are as loving and accepting as my husband are very rare. When I do find them (and I have found a few very special people in my church) I treasure them greatly.

One big problem I have is putting myself in someone else's position, imagining how they feel about something. People have asked me, "How would you feel if you were in that person's shoes?" when there has been a situation where someone was upset or angry. Well, first I think about their shoes. If their feet are smaller than mine, I think it would be uncomfortable or even painful. If they are larger, I think I would be afraid of losing the shoes because they would fall off of my feet. If they have ugly shoes or shoes that don't look comfortable, well I wouldn't want to wear them (but I wouldn't want to wear someone else's shoes anyway).

But I know what answer they are looking for, so I don't say all of that. I know that they want me to pretend to be that person and think about how I would feel if I was that person. Then I would know how that person was feeling. I try really hard, but I can't think about how it would feel to be someone else. It is like a blank wall. There is nothing there when I try to do that. I think and think and try and try, but nothing happens. I usually know the answer they expect, though and sometimes I say that. I am not sure if that is a lie because I do know the answer they want; I just don't know it because I have imagined myself as someone else as they asked. I haven't felt it.

I also don't understand the concept of "small talk." It is hard to remember all of the rules of communication. I have to remember that when someone says, "How are you?" there are three things you need to know.

1. They do not expect you to say how you really are.

2. They expect you to just say "fine."

3. They expect you to ask how they are (and not really mean it).

This is so confusing! Why ask the question if you don't want the answer? But I do my best to do right because I want to help people find Jesus. I want them to meet Him, to know Him and to be able to go to Heaven. And the best way to help them find Jesus is to show them Jesus through me. If I am a complete freak, a total alien, people will stay away from me and I will never get the chance to help them find Jesus. So because of that, I need to try to appear as normal as possible. Often it is fairly easy to do in the short term, but over an extended period of time it is extremely difficult and often trying to be "normal" for a long time causes my "deficits" to be worse, much more pronounced and noticeable.

So now I just don't try to be normal. I can't be anyone but me. My husband has helped me accept myself, just as I am. God made me this way for a reason and if I try to be someone else, I am telling God that the way He made me isn't good enough. I don't want to do that, it isn't right. So, I am just me. .

6

SHOWING GOD TO OTHERS

"Let the word of Christ dwell in you richly as you teach and admonish one another with all wisdom, and as you sing psalms, hymns and spiritual songs with gratitude in your hearts to God." Colossians 3:16

There are many times that I know God speaks through me. During those times I don't have to think at all about what is coming out of my mouth, it just comes out. I speak without pictures (except for what God shows me), without anything in my head, really. It is difficult to explain, but it is during those times that I know God is talking to someone through me so I just let Him. And always the person we are talking to says that it was just what they needed to hear. They thank me, but I try to tell them it isn't me, it is God. Sometimes they understand, sometimes they don't.

This means that I have a big responsibility, though. If these people think I am talking to them, I have to show them Jesus. I can't just say the words. It is no good if God talks through me, then I don't act as if God is in me. It is like I am saying one thing and doing something opposite (they call it "do as I say and not as I do). I understand that God is the one talking and I am the one acting, but most people don't really understand this – or they don't want to understand it. Because of this, I have to act the way that God talks through me. That way they aren't confused. I know how it feels to be confused and I don't like it at all.

I don't try to force God on people. Many times, though, the conversation will go that way, toward talking about God. They will say something or ask a question and God just pops right into the conversation. This usually leads to questions or they make statements about what they believe – or they just agree with me. Whatever happens, the conversation starts about God. That is when the words come. I don't think them, they are just there. They fill a space in my throat and pour out of my mouth. I can't explain it. Many times I say things or use words that I don't normally say and a lot of the time things come out and it is like I am really insightful and truly understand people, but I don't. It is hard to explain. The only reason I have for it is that God is talking through me.

When I am not talking, or when God is not talking through me, I try to show God to people. I try to be positive, encouraging, helpful and kind. These are broad terms and it took me a while to match the things I was doing with the right words, but these words describe it all the best.

Most of the time, I can tell when someone looks different, like if they are tired or stressed or happy (although many times I don't for sure know what the looks mean, but I can guess and sometimes I am correct). Their face looks different, the lines by their eyes are deeper or they might almost disappear. Sometimes their eyes, or around their eyes have a light (as long as I don't have to look in their eyes I don't mind looking at their eyes – but not for too long). Other times, their eyes look dead, like there is no life in them. They are talking, but their eyes don't have the light. I have been hunting and when you kill a deer their eyes look that way – dead. But I don't know what these different looks mean so I have learned to ask, "Are you OK?" This is apparently socially appropriate because no one seems to mind. I also learned that if they say, "Yeah," I say that they look a little tired but still look good. That seems to be OK too.

People can be noisy and each individual has his or her own smell. When there are several (more than two) people in a room with me, it can get so noisy and I can smell them all. The smell isn't always bad, but I do notice. The noise almost always makes me nervous. But if I am going to show people how to find God, I have to go where they are. I can't wait for them to come to me. Plus, I need a space where I am safe and comfortable, where it is dark, quiet and cool. So I usually go to them and then retreat to my space.

But if someone comes into my space, I try to be polite. Sometimes it is hard. If I am thinking about something or working or writing, they make me nervous. They talk or they stand over me. If it is someone I know doesn't like me, that just makes it worse. I know, though that it is impolite to say, "Get away from me!" but I wish they wouldn't get so close sometimes, especially the ones who are mean or don't like me.

I have encountered some people who were unkind to me, but I just try to avoid them as best I can. I don't try to be mean back to them because this seems like wasted energy and I know that Jesus wouldn't act like that. So, even if I avoid the person, when I do interact with them I try to show kindness, compassion and grace. I am not nasty back to them. I think that is a waste and that is not how Jesus wants us to treat each other.

The thing is, most people don't even realize that I have Asperger's. They say I am "shy" or "introverted." They don't realize just how lost and confused I feel in this world. I hear many normal people say that autistic people and people with Asperger's are trapped in their own world. They make it sound like a bad thing.

The truth is, I like who I am, how I think and the "world" I live in. I don't understand the normal world, but it is OK. I have learned some skills that help me navigate it. I have a job, am married, go to church and I have a few (more than two) friends (but not all people who are nice to me are my friends). Best of all, I am a Christian.

So people confuse me, but I think I probably confuse them too (some tell me that). I try to keep them from being confused or offended, but if something happens, I explain my condition the best that I can. That way we can better understand each other and our differences will not get in the way of our talks about God. I can show them God and I don't have to be normal to do that. If I had to be normal to do that, God wouldn't use me and I would never meet anyone who needed to hear what He has to say and he would never put the words in my throat. .

7

GOD'S GIFT OF ANIMALS

"All things were made through Him; and without Him was not anything made that hath been made." John 1:3

I think that animals are a very special gift that God has given us. When you bond with an animal, your spirit interlaces with theirs and they know your pain, your joy, your suffering and your peace. They may not know exactly what these things are, but they know what is bad and what is good.

I have almost always had animals around me and usually they are better than most people. They are like little children, honest, loving and trusting. You don't have to guess what they mean, they don't communicate one thing when they mean another and their needs are simple. They need food, water, shelter and companionship. My needs are simple too. I don't need the fancy house or expensive car. My home is sparsely furnished, but it is comfortable.

I have a dog, Sammie, who is such a good friend to me. When I come home she can tell how I feel. I don't know how she does it, but if I feel OK, she just comes by for a quick pat, then goes on her way. If I am feeling not so good (even if I don't show it) she stays right by me. She is very still while I pet her and she is much less hyper around me. It is as if she knows that there is a time to be hyper and a time to be calm.

Sometimes, though, she gets really excited when I come home. She jumps up on me and wants to lick me. I get a little annoyed, but I try to remember that she is just like me in some ways. She doesn't understand appropriate social behavior, just like me, only I have learned what is OK and what is not. She can learn too, I have had dogs that have learned what is the right way to behave socially and what is not. Sometimes she just forgets – so do I. In those ways, she and I are very much alike.

I know that animals don't have a soul and I know that upsets some people. But I do think that God does something special with the animals when they die. They may not go to heaven, but I think something happens because they feel and they care. They care even if they don't exactly know what they are caring about or why they care. That is what makes it all so special. They don't have to know why or what, they just do it. They feel that push and they follow it.

When I feel that push, I follow it too. Usually I don't know exactly what I am doing, why I am putting my hand on a stranger's shoulder when I don't like to touch people usually. I don't know why I am talking to someone on the subway when I am very uncomfortable talking to most people, especially strangers. But I don't have to know why or what. If God pushes me, wants me to do something, I just do it – most of the time. Sometimes I am just too scared, but I think most people are this way.

People call animals "God's creatures" but I don't really think that they are trying to start a conversation about God. However, when someone uses this term, I usually say back to them, "Yes, God is good." Sometimes I say something else about God like He created a beautiful world. They almost always agree with me.

I don't think that we came from animals, though. That is silly. There is just too much scientific evidence regarding our biology, chromosomes and gene sequences (my husband said that is enough, I should not get into all that here - I will tell you, I have found a lot of evidence that says humans most definitely did not come from monkeys - and to think that is just ludicrous!).

But even still, the life had to start somewhere and there is nothing in this world that has been able to duplicate the intricate workings of the human body (or an animal's body). They can't make many of the organs (and those they can are not 100% fail proof) and they can't make a person. They can take cells from a male human and a female human and if everything is right, a baby will grow, but no one can control the division and multiplication of cells that make up the human body. No one can direct the cells where to go and which cells make the heart, the brain, the skin. No, that is a wondrous miracle, a supernatural gift of life and that comes from God.

I would think anyone would be able to see that. To me it is clear as day (well, a day where the sky has no clouds – maybe it should be clear as a cloudless sky). I think that some people don't want to see it. I think they are afraid that if they acknowledge that God created the world, the animals and the people then they will have to change the way that they live. I think they are afraid of giving up their stuff and they will have to be more disciplined. I think they are afraid that they will become responsible for other people and not just for themselves, they will be accountable for the things that they do.

It is sort of easier to live in a world where there is no God, but it's what comes after this world that is really, really scary. I want to go to Heaven, but even if I didn't want to go to Heaven, I would still believe in God and love and respect Him. He is with me every day and helps me. He has given me so much and made me able to do things that I couldn't do without His help. When people have treated me unkindly or ignored me because they didn't understand me, He was always there. I have felt His presence and He has sent me wonderful people, like my husband or special people who have a strong understanding of autism or he sent me an animal so I could just hug and pet it and feel accepted just as I am.

8

MUSIC, LIGHT AND COLORS

"This is the day the Lord has made. We will rejoice and be glad in it." Psalm 118:24

I love music. Certain music calms and centers me. I like colors too. Just about everything has a color and it is fascinating to look at the leaves on a tree and see the different variations of green. I used to sit in the back in church and it was very distracting because I would note how many people were wearing red, how many blue, green and so forth. Then I would look at hair. I would note how many had brown hair, red hair and so on. I can't help it, I am very attracted to color (red is my favorite – sometimes I can't stop looking at it), it holds my attention and I am just drawn to it. When our church moved to the new building, though, I chose a seat toward the front. It is on the right side, second row from the front. I can concentrate much better now.

I am telling you this because I want you to understand some things about me before I tell you about how I reach God through music (or how God reaches me). See, when I hear music, I see it as ribbons of color. That is how music comes to me. Chopin, for instance, is usually very bright yellows, oranges and reds. Bach is usually more mellow with mid tone blues and blue gray. I really like the violin, but not when it screeches (I don't like it when people screech either). I like it when it's mellow, easy to listen to.

Praise music, though, has colors and images. Well, certain praise music has colors and images. I like a lot of music and I like to sing in church. During our praise and worship time is when I feel closest to God. Now, this is where it might get complicated, especially if you know something about people with Asperger's. People with AS usually don't "connect," at least not in the way normal people do. We do have relationships, even fall in love, but it is different. I don't know how, don't really understand it, but I do know that I don't have the same emotional component that the normal people I know have.

However, when I am getting close to God, something happens. He reaches down and touches me. I can feel him and sometimes I even cry (I usually don't realize I am crying until I feel that my face is wet). I will try to explain it to you but first I have to tell you that just the fact that I can feel Him and He can affect me in such a way is a miracle.

See, when I listen to the music, it carries me away. Well, not me, me, but spirit me. See, there is a place in the center of my chest where the music seems to go (it happens when I pray too). The light and colors reach from me, in that place, to God. I can feel Him reaching to me and I feel it when we are connected.

I don't raise my hands much, at least not all the way because it is distracting (I can feel my hands and arms and it distracts me. When I don't feel my hands and body I can concentrate better on my feeling of connection to God – PLEASE I wish people understood this!). This feeling that comes from my chest, the God connection feeling is my own way of raising my hands – maybe I am making the same gesture as someone who raises their hands but doing it my way in a way I understand, is not distracting and is physically comfortable for me. Maybe God is making accommodations for me. I think it is like that anyway.

So, when I am in church, what I see, especially with the music is light. We are all on or in this light. Some people are a part of the light, others are static (like a channel on TV that is not receiving a signal) and trying to connect with the light and still others have a light but are not connected to the main light and they want to be a part of the main light. I can watch the people and see it. It is interesting to watch, to see who is a part of the light because that is very beautiful. I want to be a part of the light and when I reach out to God in my special way and He reaches back, I am a part of that light. It is warm and is varying shades of amber.

When I am a part of it, I feel like there is less gravity. Not only do I feel like I am almost floating, my insides feel that way too. Many times I feel as if I am turning sideways or upside down. I can feel God around me and in me and I want to stay that way, so connected. Sometimes my legs feel like they are not going to hold me, but somehow I stay standing. It is like I am the only person in the room.

I like to go into wooded areas, especially just after it rains. All the colors are so bright. I can see the light much easier too, I guess because the rain cleans all the dirt away. Every living thing has a light around it, people, animals, trees. I think everyone at least senses this light. I think I sense things, but I don't really know what it is supposed to feel like to sense something so I am not certain. But I do see the light around things, but it isn't like they are glowing or anything, just very vibrant and luminescent. It is like I see with different eyes and they see it. It is hard to explain.

I see the physical world with my physical eyes. They are blue. But I see other things with different eyes. I don't know what color they are; I haven't seen them but I know they are there. Maybe they do not have a color. I think that they allow me to see music as color, though. And I think that they are also a part of how I connect to God.

I used to think that everyone experienced the world like I do. Now I know that isn't true. But just because I see things differently and experience things differently doesn't mean that they are wrong or less than what normal people see and experience. It's just a different view, like I'm looking from a different window. .

9

MY HISTORY

"Wherefore if any man is in Christ, he is a new creature: the old things are passed away; behold, they are become new."
2 Corinthians 5:17

I have made mistakes and I have done wrong things. I wasn't always a Christian. Jesus wasn't always my friend (although He always wanted to be). I know that I did things that were wrong and not pleasing to God, but I also know that once I asked for Him to forgive me, all of it was forgiven. The thing that bothers me is that people hold on to things forever. They hold on to the bad things that other people have done to them like they will die if they let it go. They use those experiences to become victims and to make other people victims.

A victim is someone who lets the bad things negatively affect them and the way they live in the world. A victim is bitter and mean and they never do anything more than be a victim. They use the experience (or experiences) that made them a victim to hurt others. They use the experience as an excuse to be mean and hurtful and abusive and turn other people into victims just like themselves.

A survivor, though, is someone who turns the bad things around into something positive and good. They may use the experience to help others or use it to strengthen their own faith. They turn it around by being kind to others and they don't try to victimize other people. I am a survivor.

I have been through a lot.

I won't talk about it too much here; this is not the place for it. All I will say is that there have been several (more than two) people in my life who have said terrible things to me. They told me that I would never be anything useful and that I would never be happy. They told me that no one would ever love me. They told me I was nothing, nobody, not special. They told me that when people close to me found out how I "really was" they would leave me. They said I could not be loved. For a long time I believed them. Now I know that they lied.

There were also people in my life who hurt me physically. There were several (more than two) people who would get angry with me and hit me or grab me. I would have bruises and cuts. They would try and try to hurt me. They hit me, punched me, kicked me, choked me and threw things at me. They held me down so I was trapped, locked me in closets or the bathroom and would not let me out. They said they wished I was dead and they said they wanted to kill me or hurt me. I think they were trying to get inside, to my spirit and my mind, but they couldn't. No one can reach that far into a person unless that person lets them. I would not let them.

When I was in school, there were some kids who were mean to me (most just ignored me – and even as an adult people mostly ignore me). They called me names. I tried to just fit in and pretend I was normal. I tried to talk, but they still didn't include me in their conversations or games. I didn't really have many friends, only two that I can think of. I think some people did try to reach out to me, but social interaction was very hard for me. Mostly, they just left me alone. The worst part, though, was when they would choose teams for a game. I was always the last person to be picked, then the team captains would often fight over who had to take me. Even then I knew I wasn't wanted. It was not a good feeling.

I can understand some why people were mean to me. My friend and my husband have both explained some things to me. They say sometimes my AS can be a challenge. They tell me that mostly the people who hurt me probably didn't know what to do with me and were probably frustrated. I don't think that is a good excuse to hurt someone or be mean to someone but maybe that is all some people know how to do.

I know that I have done wrong things and I have hurt people, but I have tried to make things right. Sometimes I hurt people's feelings without even knowing it. Sometimes

I think it would be best if I were just alone because I don't always say the right things or the things that people want to hear. My husband helps me a lot, he is very patient and kind with me, but I think sometimes I even surprise him. I might even say some things that hurt his feelings, but I never mean to do that and he understands. I know I frustrate him too though.

But although my husband is very forgiving, some people are not forgiving at all. I try to stay away from them because they hold on to the hurt and it is like a festering wound that keeps them ill and disabled.

You know, people talk about my disability, my Asperger's, but I have seen that many people disable themselves. They become disabled when they choose to not forgive, choose to hold on to the bad things people did to them. The bad things eat away at them and instead of washing it away, they hold onto those things, allowing them to gain purchase in other areas of their lives as well like relationships, personal success and even just being happy. To me, that is a bigger disability than my Asperger's because it really does disable a person. My Asperger's just poses some challenges to me and how I operate, but it does not hold me back or keep me from doing good things. That other type of disability, though, does.

One thing I do know is that I was never alone. Sometimes I didn't know that when things were happening to me, but now I do. Jesus was with me the whole time. He protected me and kept me from getting too hurt. Later, He showed me how to use my experiences to help other people.

People will hurt me, abuse me, betray me and deceive me, but my God will NEVER let me down.

10

PEACE AND HOPE AND MIRACLES

"I have told you all this so that you may have peace in me. Here on earth you will have many trials and sorrows. But take heart, because I have overcome the world." John 16:33

Jesus is always with us and angels are always guarding us. This is common knowledge if you read the Bible and listen in church. But I can feel those angels, feel God's presence, not all the time, but the incidences have increased the closer I get to God.

There are times when I actually feel angels with me. It is a feeling that I cannot describe. Words like "glorious" and "magnificent" come to mind, but they still seem to fall short of the true description of the experience. I have felt a comforting presence before, but this is different. This mighty, it is powerful, it is peaceful beyond explanation or comprehension (at least in my vocabulary).

Sometimes when I pray, I can feel angels' hands on my head. Sometimes it is just one angel, sometimes more. Sometimes they have both hands on my head, other times they have one hand on me and the other raised. They do it to my husband too, when we pray together. I don't think he realizes it though. I have thought that maybe I should tell him when it happens, but I never have. I never know what I should tell and what I should not tell. I just know that this happens and it is wonderful. It changes me and it changes him when it happens.

I feel the presence of God and it is as if the feeling, the sensation takes shape. It is palpable. It is also overwhelming, like a bright light that you can't look directly into. But the feeling is far beyond anything I have ever experienced in my life. It is filled with peace, love, protection, security and hope. It literally fills the room!

But Jesus can and will bring you peace if you only ask Him to do so. When you feel unsettled, sad, scared or upset, all you have to do is pray and He will place His healing hand upon you and you will find peace.

I am just a human, just a girl who has made a lot of mistakes, but Jesus still takes the time to minister to me. I am far from perfect, but you don't have to be perfect to get Jesus' attention. You don't even have to be "good." All you have to do is want Jesus to come into your life, want Him to bring you peace and hope. The changes that take place when He enters your heart, if you are sincere when you ask, will happen pretty much on their own. You just have to want it, want Him.

When it happens, when Jesus comes into your live, things will change. Things that you once enjoyed, that may not have necessarily been good or right, will begin to have a tinge of guilt attached. You will find that your conscience is tugged when you do things that are not pleasing to God. Even if you did not know of these things before, the awareness will come as a sixth sense, so to speak. You will begin to "just know" and you will find yourself questioning actions and events and situations.

Or they just won't hold the same appeal or satisfaction any longer. You just won't want those things any longer.

The Bible is the best place to find the answers. Church is another best place. If you are looking for peace and hope, there is only one answer, only one source. You may find solace in worldly things, but it is temporary and fleeting. Those things are not dependable and they often do not point you in the direction that leads to everlasting life. They usually don't point to Heaven. No person or thing can take the place of God in your life. And none should.

Faith is vital if you are going to survive. You have to develop a strong, unshakable faith in God and believe that He will see you through anything. Of course, the only way to develop that is to go through difficult times with Him. Each time you reach to Him when you are hurting or are in trouble, your faith will grow stronger. I have learned to put my trust in God, no matter what. Sometimes a situation will look bleak and it is hard to keep my focus, but deep down I know that God will take care of me. The really hard part is when I know or suspect that the outcome is not what I want. That is really hard, but I accept it and it always works out just right – or better. Always.

It is important to keep your focus on God during times of crisis. As I have mentioned, I have been through some terrible, heartbreaking things. Sometimes I kept God in my sights, sometimes I did not. But in both I learned valuable lessons. When God is in your sights, you have a way, a path, a course of action. You have protection. Your way won't be easier, not likely anyway, but you will find more peace and growth. Instead of looking at yourself in your crisis, look at God in your crisis. It isn't about how you are in your difficult times, but how God is in your difficult times. When you stop and look, you will see that He is working miracles.

Peace is a miracle. Hope is a miracle. The fact that you woke up this morning is a miracle. The fact that this book has found its way into your hands is a miracle. Even if things don't seem to go the way you want, God will direct them in such a way that you will grow. He will use the hard times, the painful times, the times when you feel that the world is against you to help you grow and draw closer to Him. When the devil wants to beat you down and separate you from God, God will be there to comfort you. You won't be miraculously delivered, not likely anyway. After all, God let Moses wander in the wilderness for 40 years!

But the wilderness (difficult times) makes you strong and increases your faith. God will provide for you. When you start to look, you will see that you have what you need. It may not be ideal or exactly what you want and it may not come in the form you desire or expect, but it will come. And it will be right. Even if you are homeless, destitute and you feel alone, God is there. Praise Him in your suffering. All you have to do is cry out to Him.

I know that is hard. I have been through a lot of terrible things in my life. I have often felt alone. I have lived in abject poverty and in situations that were worse than that. But God was there. I have had some very painful times, but once I learned to reach out to God, He was always there. The Holy Spirit soothed me and helped me find peace. He did not take away the source of the pain and the attacks occurred again and again, but with God seeing me through I was better equipped to handle the situation. That is beyond miracles.

If we never had hard times we would never grow. If we never had to go out looking for something more, we might never find the gifts that God has for us. Sometime tragedy will turn your focus to another area or allow you to see things that you couldn't see before. I am not saying that God causes tragedy, but I am saying that He uses it. How is He using the crisis times in your life? .

11

PRAYER

"Don't worry about anything; instead, pray about everything. Tell God what you need, and thank Him for all He has done." Phillipians 4:6

This is a really important section.

I hear a lot of people talk about prayer, but I don't think many of them quite know the power of it. See, prayer is your way of talking to God. You can go to Him with anything. There is a proper format that you should use for praying – but not for every prayer. You can also just talk to Him. I do it all the time. I will talk about the proper format for prayer in a moment. First, though, I need to tell you something more important. I need to tell you how to make your prayer life more fruitful (productive) and your prayers stronger.

Speak up. Words are powerful and when you pray aloud you bring the words to life. There is great power in the spoken word. Praying aloud weaken's the devil's influence and efforts to affect and influence us. It puts up a barrier between you and the devil and makes it harder for him to get to you.

"Death and life are in the power of the tongue, and those who love it will eat its fruit." Proverbs 18:21

Pray in faith. You have to expect and believe that God is going to answer your prayers. Expect miracles.

"And all things you ask in prayer, believing, you will receive." Matthew 21:22 Believe it. When you ask God for something BELIEVE IT, claim it in faith. No matter what others say, thank God for answering your prayers, regardless of how He answers it (sometimes it may not be what you expect or want, but He always knows what is right). Every time doubt or uncertainty or fear creep in, begin praying, thanking God for answering your prayers.

Understand God's time. God doesn't always work in our time. In fact, He hardly ever works in the time we expect. But He works in the time that is best for us. So, when you are praying for something, don't give God a timeline.

Be humble. I admit, I have a difficult time understanding humility, but I do know that part of it is not being proud and not wanting a bunch of silly stuff. Status symbol cars and big, fancy houses are not really what you should be asking for. There's nothing wrong with having that stuff if God has blessed you with it, but it should not be your focus, your primary desire.

Recognize answered prayers. Sometimes God doesn't answer our prayers the way that we want or expect Him to. He always knows better what we need and if we are asking for something that may not be good for us or not quite right, He won't do it. The thing is, you have to learn to recognize that your prayers have been answered – in the way that God feels is best.

Ask that God's will be done. Sometimes, we humans have a little trouble putting God's will before our own. But it isn't up to us. We have to stop asking from our worldly perspective, our own desires and points of view and let God do what He KNOWS is right. We have to not only ask that God's will be done, but also accept it (and that is sometimes very hard). Come to Him with a clean spirit. When you come to God, especially when you are praying for someone else, you should first ask Him to forgive your sins and you should forgive those who have wronged you. Approach God with a clean spirit by confessing your sins and asking for forgiveness.

"And whenever you stand praying, forgive, if you have anything against anyone, so that your Father also who is in heaven may forgive you your trespasses." Mark 11:25

Glorify God – always.

The Bible tells us to "pray without ceasing" and some people believe that this means they are to pray all the time – consciously pray. I think that may be true, but only partly true. I think that once you reach a certain communion with

God, a certain closeness; that your spirit prays. I think that your spirit can pray continuously even if your mind is not necessarily conscious of it.

I find that I do this. I will be going about my daily tasks at work or at home and realize that my spirit is praying, praising or just connecting with God. Sometimes it is in actual words like a dialogue (and sometimes I find myself actually saying things out loud), other times it's pictures and still other times it's songs. I do this without conscious thought, but it is still praying and still praising God. I believe that once you reach a certain level of a relationship with God, it just happens naturally. I think that we were designed that way, to praise Him and communicate with Him regularly.

I still think that you need to have some form of organized, more formal prayer each day. My husband and I pray together in the mornings. Often, before I leave our home, I walk through the house, from room to room, praying for courage to face the challenges of the day, strength to endure whatever obstacles may come into my path and protection for the house (house meaning the structure as well as our family, including our dog!).

My husband is much more organized with his prayer than I am, but I am learning. He gave me the following prayer template which is good to follow when you want to pray in a more organized and maybe even formal manner:

Praise

To know His will and do His will (and have a good attitude – that's the hard part sometimes)

Provision - Fulfilling your needs

Forgiveness for our sins (those known and not know – and the wisdom to recognize the unknown sins)

Pray for your enemies

Protection from temptation

His way of explaining it sounds much better, but this is the way I understand it so this is how I am giving it to you.

I love the quiet. Sometimes I just sit in the quiet and listen. Many times I can hear God, I can feel Him move. And sometimes God stands before me, touches me and talks to me. Sometimes He sends His angels to minister to me. I can't describe those experiences – I don't have the words for it. All I can say is that it is bigger than anything, overwhelming and powerful. I can't begin to describe the feeling. It is beyond words.

12

TOUCHING GOD

Jesus replied, "I am the bread of life. Whoever comes to me will never be hungry again. Whoever believes in me will never be thirsty." John 6:35

It is possible to touch God, I do it all the time. Well, I don't do it all the time, but I do it a lot of the time, especially when I pray. I believe that a person's spirit is not the same shape as their body, maybe not even the same size. I believe this because when I pray in tongues (praying in the spirit) or when God talks through me (which is in my spirit, not my physical body), the place where He puts the words is different from where the words are when I speak physically. The words are still in me, but not in me. It is hard to explain.

Sometimes, when my husband and I are praying, I can see God placing His hands on our heads. Sometimes He places both hands on my husband's head, sometimes on mine, sometimes on both of us. Sometimes it's angels who do it. I don't see this with my physical eyes, but I do see it with the eyes of my spirit. He is like a great golden white light and I see Him with us, touching us. I feel something different too; usually I feel very peaceful and focused. But the feeling part is a little confusing to me sometimes. I do often feel a presence.

What I see through those eyes, the eyes of my spirit, are much easier to believe and much more truthful. My physical eyes will deceive me sometimes. I may think I saw something that I did not. I may see an expression on a person and not understand it. However, when I am seeing through the eyes of my spirit, I always understand it. Sometimes I talk to my husband about it, ask questions, but I do have a good understanding of it, even when it comes to people.

God speaks to each of us in ways we understand. All we have to do is stop and listen. We all touch God. Some people don't realize it and some don't want to think about it, but it is true. Even people who don't believe in God or don't want to believe in God are still touched by Him. He will show himself to them (in different ways) but a lot of times they choose not to see it. He reaches out to them, but they choose not to take His hand. If only they would reach back, then they would know.

When I pray, I reach out from that place in my chest. My spirit reaches up to Him and He reaches back to me. It is like we hold hands, but more. There is an intertwining of my spirit with His. He fills me up and holds me up. He puts understanding, wisdom and words in my mind. He puts energy in my spirit like charging a battery. It makes me feel like there is no gravity. Sometimes I feel like I am turning upside down, but my body stays in the same position.

Sometimes, when I raise my hands (I don't raise them all the way, it is distracting because I can feel them) I feel God holding my hand. I can feel His hand in mine. It is warm and strong. It also makes me feel safe but also strong.

God is very real, very living. If you want to feel Him, experience Him, know Him, all you have to do is reach out to Him. I talk to Him a lot, especially about helping other people. He lets me know when things are OK or not OK. He communicates with me and answers me when I call on Him. If you call out to Him, He will answer you too.

When God talks to you, it will be in different ways. Sometimes you will just know something and you will know that it came from God. Usually you will know because it will be knowledge that you don't know how you know or it will be words and phrases you don't use. Other times, He will use the people you encounter, material you read, shows you watch, music you listen to and sometimes He will intermingle these with events that will cause you to know without a doubt that God has spoken to you. All you have to do is listen but listen with your spirit because he may not always use the ears that are on your physical body.

I feel much more in touch with the spiritual part of myself than the physical part. I think this may have something to do with the Asperger's. My physical body feels clunky and awkward a lot of the time, the physical sensations I have are distracting. The sensory issues I have compound those distractions as lights that are too bright, sounds that grate on my nerves and material that scrapes against my skin. But when I close my eyes and am perfectly still, all that falls away and I am my complete spiritual self. At that time, God reaches down and touches me. It is when I am most open and I know.

I have learned how to listen to God at other times and I am able to respond to his prompts, words and calls. For years I have carried a small notebook and pen with me at all times because I am very prone to having sudden insight and feeling a pressing, urgent need to write it all down. I can't explain it except to say that when I get these feelings it is as if I will explode if I don't write.

I may not be thinking of anything in particular, but suddenly the warmth will come and things will start flowing. Then I start writing. I have filled pages in a matter of minutes, not remembering what I have written, but when I go back it is perfectly understandable. It is also usually above my capabilities in understanding on certain levels. Many times I understand it once I have written it, but prior to that I had no understanding of the material. Other times, I know that the message wasn't meant for me and I don't need to understand it, so I just pass it on in whatever way I am prompted to do so.

I had not understood that this was a direct communication with God. For years I just thought I was getting "flashes of inspiration." I refused to recognize the obvious pattern – during the times I was closest to God, the "flashes" were more frequent and intense. When I was turned from God or not focused on Him, the "flashes" were less frequent or nonexistent (or turned almost completely on me all of the time). As my walk with God has become more intense and my relationship with Him has grown of late, the "flashes" occur pretty much on a daily basis. He talks, I write, sometimes for hours.

Even as you read this, there is no doubt in my mind that God has placed something in here just for you. He has directed this project from the start and in fact had placed this on my heart long before I begin to put the words on paper. I was resistant and afraid. What if I did something wrong or started putting my own words in here instead of God's? Then I realized that He wanted me to interject my own words here, that it was necessary. As you read this, as you have read this, you will see two distinctly different types of writing. You will hear my voice as I talk to you through the Asperger's. You will also hear God's voice as he speaks through me. Maybe you will begin to understand a little (or a lot) of both.

So, if this reads as if it were written by two different hands, it is because it was. But God had to do it that way so that you would know He was guiding this, authoring those parts. If it was the same throughout, you would think it was all just me and you couldn't see the wonder of it, the miracle. As you read this, pay attention to each voice for each has a purpose. My own voice will give you some insight into me, into Asperger's. God's voice will bring to you the messages that He wants you to hear. Yes, they will be intertwined at times, but even as you read this you are touching God.

When you pray, forget about your physical body and reach out with your spirit to God. It is easy to do this, just close your eyes and find that place in you where your spirit is overflowing. You will find the door if you just close your eyes and look for it. Then let that consciousness take you before God.

If you feel far away from God, all you have to do is ask Him to come to you. Tell Him that you want a close, personal relationship with Him. The key, though, is to be sincere. You really have to want it and for the right reasons. God doesn't do silly parlor tricks – don't insult Him by requesting something like that. If you need to see Him, He will show Himself to you in the way He sees fit.

Some days I feel down, discouraged because of my condition. Some days the Asperger's feels like a great weight around my neck, dragging me down to the bottom of the sea. Some days I feel so lost and alone, so useless and in the way, but God reminds me that HE made me – just as I am. Some days he tells me through my husband, sometimes through scripture, movies, whatever seems to have my immediate attention.

People ignore me a lot and treat me like I am invisible. I won't say that on many days that is exactly how I wish to be, but some days I want people to reach out to me. I don't feel comfortable reaching out to people on many days because I don't want to bother them. Now I won't say that I don't reach out first, because when God calls on me to minister to someone, it is sometimes necessary for me to make the first move. But when I need to be ministered to, I have a hard time asking for it, reaching out to someone to get it. God is always there, though and He touches me, comforts me when the people seem to have forgotten me.

God never forgets me and He won't forget you.

13

THE STORMS

"God is our refuge and strength, a very present help in trouble. Therefore will not we fear, though the earth be removed, and though the mountains be carried into the midst of the sea; though the waters thereof roar and be troubles, though the mountains shake with the swelling thereof. Selah." Psalms 46:1-3

My life seems like it has been a series of storms. By storms I mean difficult times; times where things worked against me to crush my spirit. I know this because our pastors have talked several times about storms. They also call it the wilderness or desert when you have difficult times. But while the words are different, the meaning is the same. It describes a time when the devil creates situations that discourage you or try to prevent you from doing God's will or what He wants you to do.

Jesus is the only reason that I can get through the storms in my life.

Every time I can stand a little straighter and press on instead of curling into a ball and covering my head while I scream (which is what I really want to do sometimes) I know that Jesus has touched me. He has covered that gaping wound in my heart with His own hand.

Jesus has promised each of us that He will help us through the storms in our lives. He is always there, waiting to assist and comfort, but most of the time we have to ask him to step in, to intervene. It is a lot like our government system of federalism. The federal government is the most powerful, at the head, but it defers to the states, giving them authority over their own bodies. In times of crisis, the federal government will step in only when the state requests it. Our relationship with God is much like that. He is like the federal government and we are the states. He waits for us to request His help, His presence, His comfort.

"Give all your worries and cares to God, for He cares about you." 1 Peter 5:7

When you reach out to Him and ask for His help, He will respond. He can bring peace to a troubled heart, stillness to an unsettled mind and healing to broken hearts and broken bodies. There is absolutely nothing He cannot do. What is really cool about this set up, that doesn't occur in government is that someone else can call on God for you. They can act as a bridge and bring God into your situation. But we still have to remember that when God works, He does so in His own time.

I have a friend I knew when we were kids. Now we have reconnected online and we email now and then. She was going through a difficult time with her husband, they were on the brink of a divorce. One evening her husband was in a terrible car accident and was unconscious. She posted on FaceBook and many of her friends began posting words of encouragement, telling her that they were praying for her. I read them for a couple of days, read her updates when she went in to see him.

Then one morning I felt led to pray for the couple. I couldn't seem to get them out of my head. So that morning as my husband and I prayed, I began praying for my friend and her husband. I prayed for healing of his body, but also for healing of both of their hearts. I began to pray for healing for both of them, for healing so that they could repair and rebuild their marriage. Now, I did this strictly following God. I did not really know their situation, but He had placed it on my heart to pray specifically for this other type of healing in addition to the physical healing that the husband needed.

Then God led me to write words of faith and distinct guidance on how she should proceed now that the prayer had been set in motion. I told her that I had prayed for her husband and God said He would heal him and each of their hearts and their marriage, but now she had to CLAIM IT IN FAITH. She had to accept the truth, speak the truth, speak it as truth. Each time someone spoke in a negative way or in a way that was contrary to the message God was giving her, she was to begin praising God and thanking Him for the things He was doing in their lives.

Later that morning, I received word that he was conscious, communicating with her, crying and reaching out to her. He indicated that he wanted to renew their wedding vows. By that afternoon the doctors were able to remove his breathing tube and he was asking for ice – all the while keeping his wife nearby.

God is good.

So sometimes you may be called upon to help others through their storms (difficult times). God may appoint you to be a messenger to deliver news of all that He is doing in a life. Sometimes He will send someone to minister to you, to help you. Sometimes He will come to you in your hour of need and just hold you close.

In fact, although times of crisis are not necessarily pleasant, they can be the times that you are drawn closest to God. When all else is stripped away, God will step in and do wonderful things in your life. When I have been utterly alone, when everyone has abandoned me and hurt me, God has come to me and shown me that he is ever-present. He has used these times to teach me how to listen and how to obey Him when He speaks to me.

"For our present troubles are small and won't last very long. Yet they produce for us glory that vastly outweighs them and will last forever!" 2 Corinthians 4:17 .

14

ON BEING CONTENT

"So if we have enough food and clothing, let us be content." 1 Timothy 6:8

I don't understand some people who have a need to always have more and more. They are not content with what they have, but always want a bigger house or more expensive car. God provides us with the things that we need, and if He is doing that, why can't we just be happy?

I don't think there is anything wrong with having a big house or expensive car (although that is not something I would want), but some people make those things their God. Their desire for those things, the things they don't have and don't really need, becomes bigger and more important than anything else, including God.

And their heart never really finds peace. They are never really happy.

I don't have a lot, but I don't really want a lot. I have my books, but I really don't own that much. I like comfortable and easy. I like simple. I am not a fancy person. I used to try to be a fancy person, but it never really felt right. Now I am really me.

I think that other people worry way too much about what other people think of them. This makes their heart knot all up and they try to do things to make people like them or think highly of them. You can't make anyone think or do anything, though. People are people.

But people still get stuff and do things to make others think highly of them. What does it matter, really? I mean, if someone only likes you because you have a big, fancy, expensive car or you live in a million dollar home, what kind of friend are they? That doesn't seem very stable to me. If someone only likes you because you have stuff, then what happens if you suddenly don't have that stuff? You will be all alone, no friends and no stuff. That doesn't seem like a very pleasant place to be.

Sometimes it isn't about what others think, though, it is about being afraid. Some people are afraid of running out of stuff, being without something or not having what they need (or think that they need). What they don't realize is that God makes sure that we have everything that we need.

Maybe it all comes from fear. People are afraid of being alone, so they get a lot of stuff to make them seem like something special (they are warped because they think that having stuff makes them special – they are already special) and they think that will make others like them. That way, they won't be alone, so they think.

I think that discontent is rooted in two distinct areas, fueled by fear. These areas are:

Expectations of self

Expectations of others

People use their lives, careers, relationships and possessions to raise themselves up. They become discontented when they feel that they fall short in these areas. They also can become discontented when they place expectations on other people and those people do not live up to those expectations. They measure their lives by things of the flesh. What they don't realize is that those things don't matter. Things of the flesh, stuff, will rot and break; it can be stolen or destroyed. People can devalue it and it can go out of style. These events will keep you on a path of always trying to acquire new stuff. You will always be restless in that area, always looking, always seeking, always wanting, always longing and your thirst will never be quenched because your spirit is parched.

What you have to do is find a measure in your life that is not affected by outer sources. God is the only answer for that. Only God can provide a measure for you that no one else can ever touch. Realize that "good enough" is actually good enough. God will give you what you need. He may give you more, but you need to learn to be happy with what

He does give you because He knows what is best for you. He knows what lies deep within your heart and what will heal the wounds there, close the gaps of loneliness and despair. He knows how to minister to you in ways you can't imagine.

Your stuff will only take you so far, but when you take your eyes off of the stuff and focus on God, things will begin to change. Your world will get brighter; the light will scare away the shadows of doubt, anger, sorrow, despair, hopelessness, emptiness and restlessness. You will no longer feel a need to search because you will have found the answer to everything.

It is OK to have things, nice things. There is nothing wrong with wealth or possessions. There is, however, grave danger when you cross the line and the things you possess begin to possess you. When you become so wrapped up on acquiring more and more things and your focus falls from God to the things, you are starving your spirit, your heart will wither. God is the ONLY REMEDY for that. There is NOTHING else that can do it. .

15

ON FORGIVENESS

"Judge not and ye shall not be judged; condemn not and ye shall not be condemned; forgive and ye shall be forgiven."
Luke 6:37

I asked my husband what forgiveness feels like.

My husband is my guide in this world. I know that God sent him to me to help me navigate this confusing, noisy world. Sometimes my questions amuse him. He tells me that sometimes he gets frustrated, but most of the time he is amused. He is almost always patient with me, though. But no matter what I ask, he tries to answer me and most of the time he doesn't even get shocked.

So when I asked him what forgiveness felt like, he was quiet for a moment. I know (because I know him) that this is when he is thinking, usually to decide on the best way to explain something to me. I am not stupid, but I don't understand most feelings or emotions. I wanted to know what forgiveness felt like so I could know if I had forgiven someone who had hurt me.

He told me that forgiveness doesn't necessarily mean that you forget what someone has done to you. He said it does mean that you "let it go," meaning that it no longer holds you back or keeps you from moving forward.

So I decided to explore the gift of forgiveness. I wanted to see what God has to say about it and how we should act when someone wrongs us. The pain, bitterness and resentment that comes from not forgiving will weigh heavily on your heart and keep you from growing, from getting closer to God.

It's funny. I love God with my whole heart. I strive every day to do the things He wants me to do. I want to do His will and fulfill the purpose that He has for me. But this close walk with God does not guarantee that I won't still have struggles. It does not mean that I won't feel resentment and bitterness. It does not mean that I won't grabble with the act of forgiving someone for hurting me. This is something all Christians face. We all are told by God that we are to be loving and forgiving. Sometimes, though, that is extremely difficult.

I used to think that being a Christian was the easiest thing in the world. Now I know that in many ways it is far harder than not being a Christian. But the rewards are far greater and the peace is incomparable. He blesses me every single day, even on days that seem dark (on those days I have to take off my blinders to see them). God is so very good to me.

Proverbs 21:21 tells us, "Whoever pursues righteousness and unfailing love will find life, righteousness and honor." I was pretty sure I understood this verse, but the word "righteousness" was a little confusing. I find that some words in the Bible are somewhat abstract and could even be considered subjective. It is hard for me to know just what the words mean from a God perspective. This is one of the struggles that I have with Asperger's. If something isn't straightforward or leaves any room for interpretation, I get bound in the details of the puzzle and can't see the big picture.

And don't even get me started on Jesus' parables! Fishers of men? That's makes an interesting picture in my mind. My husband has patiently discussed many of those parables with me (and some confusing worship songs too – salt of the world?). I go to him with, I am sure, some bizarre questions. We have talked about the man who built his house on sand and the one who built his house on rock. I now know (after lengthy discussion) that the "house" is the man's character, his core, his faith. The "sand" is symbolic of the things in life that are not stable – money , possessions, anything that is not of God. The "rock" is God. When the man focused on God and made Him the core of his being, then he could withstand the hard times in his life.

So, the word "righteousness" puzzled me. It means "being moral, having virtue, being right," but those things have no concrete meaning in my world. Everyone has a different definition of "right." I think, though, that too many people look at these words from a human perspective and not from a God perspective. When we look at these things from Jesus' point of view (in the Bible), we can see that the definition is much clearer – and much harder to carry out. Of course, God knows we can't be perfect like Jesus, but He does expect us to do our best.

I have children and I have told them to do their best in school or other things that they were doing. Sometimes they did their best and sometimes they did not. Sometimes they did just enough to get by. Face it; doing your best, your true best, requires effort. Even great effort at times. So, when God tells us to do something, like love everyone with unfailing love and to be righteous and forgive those who hurt us, he is also saying, "I don't expect you to be perfect or to do it perfectly, but I do expect you to do your best."

Do you give your best to God or do you do just enough to get by? Doing your best for God is really hard sometimes, at least for me, especially when He wants me to love and forgive someone who has hurt me badly.

I also know that harboring ideas of revenge, wishes of poetic justice or anything like that is NOT of God. I think it might be normal for humans to want a person who has wronged them to pay a price. I know that many movies, TV shows and books promote this mentality, but I can tell you most assuredly, that this is NOT of God, not what He wants us to want or pursue.

The way I see revenge is that it gives the people who have hurt you even more power. When you seek revenge, you have let the person who wronged you break you. It lets them know that they have broken you. Instead of rising above it and acting in a Godly way, you have given in to your baser instincts, those that are of the flesh and not of God.

Revenge and all the messy emotions that go along with it (anger, rage, hatred, bitterness) do nothing more than stir up more trouble. Job 4:8, "My experience shows that those who plant trouble and cultivate evil will harvest the same."

Then you are no better than your tormenter. You can't control how others act or how they treat you, but you can control how their actions affect you. You can control how you react to them. And that is where you choose the way of the flesh or the way of God. Proverbs 21:21 says, "Whoever pursues righteousness and unfailing love will find life, righteousness and honor." So, forgiveness is definitely of God. .

16

BEING THE FRINGE

"Instead, you must worship Christ as Lord of your life. And if someone asks you about your Christian hope, always be ready to explain it." 1 Peter 3:15

There are people who will look at you as a Christian and say that you are not sincere. They will say that you are "putting on a front." That happened to me. Someone, actually several someones, accused me of that. These were people who were close to me, people I cared about, loved, and some have even been on my journey with me as I drew closer to God. I know that those were demonic influences leading those people to say those things, but that doesn't make it any easier.

I do have a past, as I have told you. I have done things I shouldn't have done. Some of the people in my life can't move past that. They choose to remain mired in unpleasant

83

things as if pain is a dear friend. What I have seen, though, is that the more they hold on to pains of the past, the more skewed reality becomes to them. The truth of the painful events melts away and reality is embellished with lies and deceit until the original story is gone and all that remains is a work of fiction. Then their fiction becomes their reality.

People in my own life have done this to me, twisting facts and including "recounting" events that never even happened. But I know two things regarding this and I hold onto these truths:

God knows the truth and He has forgiven me for any sins I have committed

God will not hold against me those things He has already forgiven me for GOD DOES NOT HOLD GRUDGES! People do. If you have asked God to forgive you and you were sincere, then He has forgiven you. It is past; it is done. It will haunt you no longer so don't give it power by ruminating on it. These are demonically driven events (don't think that just because you are a Christian that you are not above demonic influence – that is very naïve. You are even more prone to attacks – you just have a better arsenal for combat). To think of them, to be consumed with guilt even after you have been forgiven is destructive and not productive to having a close, personal relationship with God and living a Christian life.

People will think what they want to think. You can't change that. But if you are right with God, then you are OK. If they see your grace and mercy even as they condemn you, ridicule you, attempt to make you doubt your relationship with God, then you have planted a seed. It may take root right then, it may take years, or it may never happen (if they are indeed a barren land – not receptive to God). What matters is that you show them Jesus' face at all times, whether they reach out to Him or not.

That is the key to being the fringe. God is the light of the world and it is our job as Christians to go out into the world and show God to the people.

Know, though, that even though you may have changed; even though you are close to God, the people in your life may still try to hold you to your old self. When you talk to them about Christ, about being a Christian, about having a close relationship with God, they may not want to listen. They may even tell you that, given your past and the things you have done that you are not the best person to be talking about those things. They may even try to remind you of things you have done in your past that are ungodly so that they can discredit you as a Christian and make you less of an authority to speak to them on things of a Christian or godly matter.

Don't let that deter you. People will try to steer you off of the topic and try to discredit you when you talk to them about things that prick their conscience. When they start to feel guilt, they will attack the person who is causing the guilt. If you are holding up their actions for examination and they feel ashamed for their behavior, then they will try to discredit you so that in their own mind you are no better than they are, thus unable to make them feel shame or guilt because your past actions are just as bad or worse than what they themselves are doing.

Being the fringe, the light, being a Christian doesn't mean that your life will always be easy. In fact, in some ways it is actually more difficult. The deeper you get, the closer you get to God, the harder the devil will work to steer you off of your path. He will use whatever means he can, whatever people he can influence, to distract you and corrupt you. His one desire is to come between you and God and destroy that relationship.

Even other Christians may do things that are ungodly. They will make mistakes – all humans make mistakes. They will do things that are not pleasing to God. However, as a Christian, it is up to you to be an influence, to set an example for others to follow. You won't be perfect all the time either. The best you can do is help those who fall instead of passing judgment.

It is our job to minister to people. We should reach out to them, help them, encourage them. However, reaching out, helping and encouraging people when you see them at church is not enough. It is easy to talk to someone when you encounter them at church. You are both in the same place, you don't have to go out of your way to minister to them. However, when you go out of your way, take the time to minister to them outside of church, then you will make a stronger impact. Do more than to just get by, go above and beyond to reach people.

Being Christian, being godly is not always easy and it can make you subject to mistreatment, pain and even suffering, but the rewards are great. God will honor those who earnestly strive to live a godly life, who try to be what God wants them to be and do His will.

It isn't easy, but it is so worth it. .

17

GOING TO HEAVEN

Then Peter said unto them, "Repent and be baptized every one of you in the name of Jesus Christ for the remission of sins and ye shall receive the gift of the Holy Ghost." Acts 2:38

Some people call this part "eternal life" or "being saved," but those just make confusing pictures in my head for me. And "going to be with Jesus" is just, well, silly because you can be with Jesus anywhere. You don't have to die and go to Heaven to be with Jesus. So, I prefer to say "going to Heaven" because that is exactly what it is.

The only way to Heaven is through Jesus. You have to know Him; have to have a personal relationship with Him. You can't get to Heaven by just being a good person and doing good things. It really bothers me that so many people actually believe that!

There are three things necessary to get to Heaven:

You have to repent, confess your sins to God and ask Him to forgive you and save you (you have to do this on an ongoing basis – have a relationship with God and you have to foster it like you would any other relationship, nurturing it, making it grow deeper and stronger)

You have to be baptized in the Holy Spirit (speaking in tongues is a sign of this)

You have to be baptized by immersion in water in the name of Jesus Christ (this is very important!)

Now, you have to repent. This means that you have to ask God to forgive you for your sins. You do have to do your best to live a godly life, the way Jesus wants you to live, but it is much more than that. When you truly repent and ask Jesus to take over your life, He will give you the gift of the Holy Spirit. When you commune with God, you will receive a sign, something tangible or audible, something that will let you know that you are definitely communicating with God.

You will feel His presence, He will fill you. You will feel God moving. And when He gives you the gift of the Holy Spirit, you will speak in other tongues. Now, I have known some people who did not grow up in this faith and they freak out when they hear this. Some even say it isn't real or is demonic. That is so far from the truth! Speaking in tongues is the result, is evidence of receiving the gift of the

Holy Ghost, the true mark of "spirit filled Christians." It is in the Bible.

There does not need to be an interpreter as some people mistakenly believe. There are different types of speaking in tongues. This one is as evidence of being baptized in the Holy Spirit. Sometimes someone will speak in tongues and someone will interpret, but other times it is just between the person and God, especially when you can't find the right words or don't know what to pray for. Sometimes it happens around people, like in church and other times it is in private. It is praying in the spirit and it is beautiful.

There are a lot of times that I wake up in the middle of the night and I am speaking in tongues. It happens when I am brushing my hair, driving in my car, walking in the grocery store, just whenever the spirit moves through me. The important thing is to yield to it, to submit to God.

That is hard for me sometimes, especially when I am in a place where there are a lot of distractions. I can't focus on God and what He is doing through me. I can't focus on the Holy Spirit moving through me. The words may come, but then they are lost. I do much better when it is quiet and there is nothing to distract me. Maybe it is because I am new to it all. I hope that is the case. A lot of times I start analyzing what is happening and it stops. It is like something you can't look at directly or it will disappear.

This (praying/speaking in tongues) is necessary if you want to go to Heaven because it is proof that you have received the gift of the Holy Spirit which the Bible says is required to get into Heaven (receiving the gift of the Holy Spirit). So basically, when you receive the gift of the Holy Spirit it will happen; it isn't anything that you can make happen or that you can control. The Bible says it is so and I am not going to argue with the Bible. It frustrates me because so many people have picked apart the Bible as if they can just choose the parts that they like and throw out the parts that they don't like or that make them uncomfortable. But the Bible is the Bible, in its entirety.

So if you want to go to Heaven, you need to begin by praying and reading your Bible. Get to know God, I mean really get to know Him. That is the *only* way you will learn to know His voice when He speaks to you. Study His word but don't stop there. The next thing you are obligated to do, as a Christian is to lead others to Him. Just share your faith with others.

Once you pray and ask Jesus to forgive you of your sins and take you to Heaven when you die, if you are sincere in your faith, repent of all of your sins and actively seek the gift of the Holy Spirit you will receive it. Sometimes you don't even have to ask for it. Some people are a little afraid of this part because it means a certain amount of loss of control, but it is OK. It is wonderful.

Some people shout loudly in tongues, others sing, others barely whisper. I find myself waking in the middle of the night to pray in tongues. Sometimes I am called on by God to pray for a certain person whom He has laid on my heart and I will start in my own language but then I start praying in another one. I admit, I was a little freaked when it first happened (it happened before I was even baptized). I wasn't sure what was going on. I knew of it, my husband does it regularly when we pray, but the first time it happened to me it was just so unfamiliar.

It is much easier now and much more comfortable. Now it feels more normal and natural. It is just a much more intimate way of communicating with God. And if you want to get to Heaven, well, that is part of the package.

The important thing to understand about speaking in tongues though is that you can't control it. God will give it to you when it is your time. If you actively seek it by asking Him and praying aloud, He will give it to you. Some people, though, don't feel worthy to receive it and that hinders them. Know this: not one of us is worthy! We are all sinners and we don't deserve any of the wonderful things that God gives us. But He died for us so we could receive His blessings and gifts and eternal life. Don't let your feelings of unworthiness hold you back and keep you from the power and awe of the Holy Spirit baptism.

Now, God wants me to tell you some things about Christian life. See, last night I prayed that as I completed this book that He would guide me in this last, most crucial part. He gave me the book of Titus chapter 2. Honestly, I don't recall reading much on Titus; it is a small book consisting of only 3 chapters, but in it the Apostle Paul is giving instruction to Titus. I had not read Titus, except for a verse here and there, but when God directed me there, particularly to chapter 2, I admit, I was a little breathless when I read it. It was exactly what was needed!

So, I will paraphrase here, but I urge you to read Titus 2. Really, I urge you to read the whole Bible. But for now, this is what God wants me to tell you about living a God-filled life.

Most of what consists of a God-filled life is living it so that you set a good example for others to follow. He says that older men should be guided to live lives of temperance, dignity and wisdom, into healthy faith, love and endurance. While it says "older men," we should all strive to live in this manner.

Older women should live in reverence so that they do not become gossips or drunk. We are to be models of goodness. Younger women should be able to look, watch the older women and learn how to love their husbands and children. Women are to be virtuous and pure, keep a good house and be good wives. Young men should lead disciplined lives.

We are to live in this way so that people who see us and witness our behavior won't look down on God's message. In short, we are to set good examples for others to follow. We don't just *tell* people how to find Jesus, we *show* them. And then we show them how to live the life, walk the walk. But we are told, mostly, to show the people we are teaching all of these things by doing it ourselves. We are to be incorruptible in our teaching and our words are to be solid and sane. By setting this kind of solid, strong example, anyone who is intent on being against us or refuting the Word of God will have no ammunition. They will find nothing that is misguided or not consistent with God's word and they may even eventually become saved themselves.

We are to have and display good character that will show through our actions and will enhance the teaching of Jesus.

Salvation is available for everyone. Jesus died for our sins; he paid the ultimate price for us so that we can live in Heaven forever and ever.

We are to turn our backs on a life that is godless, one that is indulgent and filled with worldly things. Our lives should be God-filled and God-honoring. Begin without delay. You don't have to be perfect, just do your very best (truly your best) to live a Godly life.

As I read all of this, as I have been writing this, I have been dealing with a very painful situation. My very relationship with God has been attacked. The people who are doing this are close to me, related to me. It hurts, but as I completed this chapter, the one God led me to, the last verse encouraged me and gave me hope.

"These things speak and exhort and reprove with all authority. Let no man despise thee." Titus 2:15

God wanted me to tell you these things, but He also wanted me to know this. So through the things I have relayed to you from Him, I have also learned and grown. Thank you. When it is all said and done, there is a God in this world and ultimately we will each have to answer to Him. We will have to shoulder the responsibility for our own actions; no one can do that for us.

If you have asked Jesus to come into your life and forgive you of your sins, if you have been baptized in the Holy Spirit and been baptized by immersion in water in Jesus' name AND tried your best to live the way God wants you to live then you will go to Heaven. If you have not taken these steps, if you are hiding from things you have done, if you are ashamed and that shame is keeping you from coming forward before Jesus, if you are proud and that pride is preventing you from humbling yourself before God, then you will go to hell. It is that simple.

Is YOUR house in order?

"Always be full of joy in the Lord, I say it again – rejoice!" Phillipians 4:4.

WHAT'S NEXT?

I hope that this book has blessed you and spoken to you in a very personal, profound way. If you enjoyed reading this, please don't keep it to yourself. Give a copy to someone you think needs to hear one of the messages in here and let it bless them too! Feel free to contact me through my FaceBook page or by email at TheChristianAspie@gmail.com. You can also visit my website http://TheChristianAspie.com and read my blog, find resources and join the Christian Aspie Forum so we can communicate. I would love to hear from you.

God is GOOD!

Stephanie Mayberry

ABOUT THE AUTHOR

Stephanie Mayberry is a Christian author whose passion for writing has become her ministry. An active member of the ministry team at The Life Church PWC in Manassas, VA, she has given her life to God and is realizing her calling of ministry through her writing.

As an adult with Asperger's Syndrome, she ministers to other Aspies (people with Asperger's Syndrome) through her blog, The Christian Aspie and several books she has written about being a Christian with Asperger's Syndrome. She also uses her experiences as a battered wife to reach out to people who have been through abuse and help them find healing through Jesus.

But God has also impressed upon her to write other titles as well. As she says, "God writes the words, I just hold the pen."

Stephanie lives in Virginia, just outside of Washington, D.C. with her infinitely patient husband and a dog genius.

READ OTHER BOOKS
BY STEPHANIE MAYBERRY AT

https://www.amazon.com/author/stephaniemayberry

http://www.smashwords.com/profile/view/StephanieMayberry

VISIT STEPHANIE'S BLOG AT:

http://TheChristianAspie.com

CONNECT WITH STEPHANIE

Email: stephanie@thechristianaspie.com

Twitter: http://twitter.com/fotojunkie

Facebook:
http://www.facebook.com/stephanie.a.mayberry

FRINGE

Printed in Great Britain
by Amazon

22100919R00066